Celebrated Virtuosic Solos

Eight Exciting Solos for Late Elementary Pianists

Robert D. Vandall

MW00368733

(UK Exam Grade 1)

Everyone who plays the piano wants to play a piece that is impressive to an audience. Pianists are drawn to those pieces that challenge them to quickly move their fingers, hands and arms, creating sounds that move the audience to respond with wild applause and shouts of "Bravo!"

The pieces in the *Celebrated Virtuosic Solos* are meant to show off the athleticism, as well as the musicality, of the performer. My hope is that these pieces will excite students, teachers and audiences alike.

Enjoy!

Robert D. Vandall

Contents

Alfred

Water Slide

Robert D. Vandall

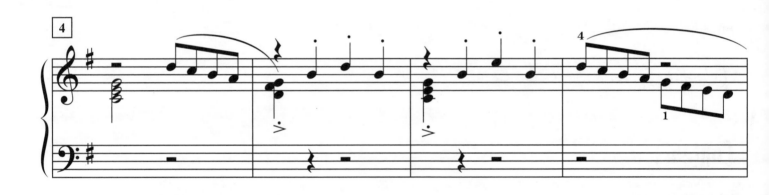

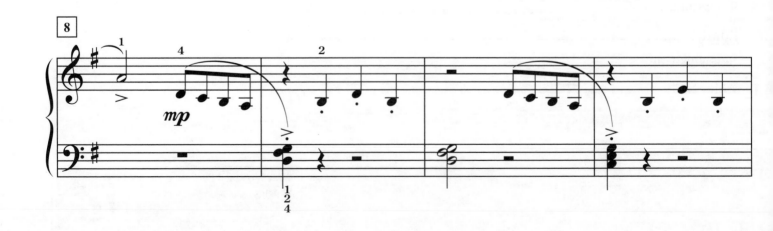

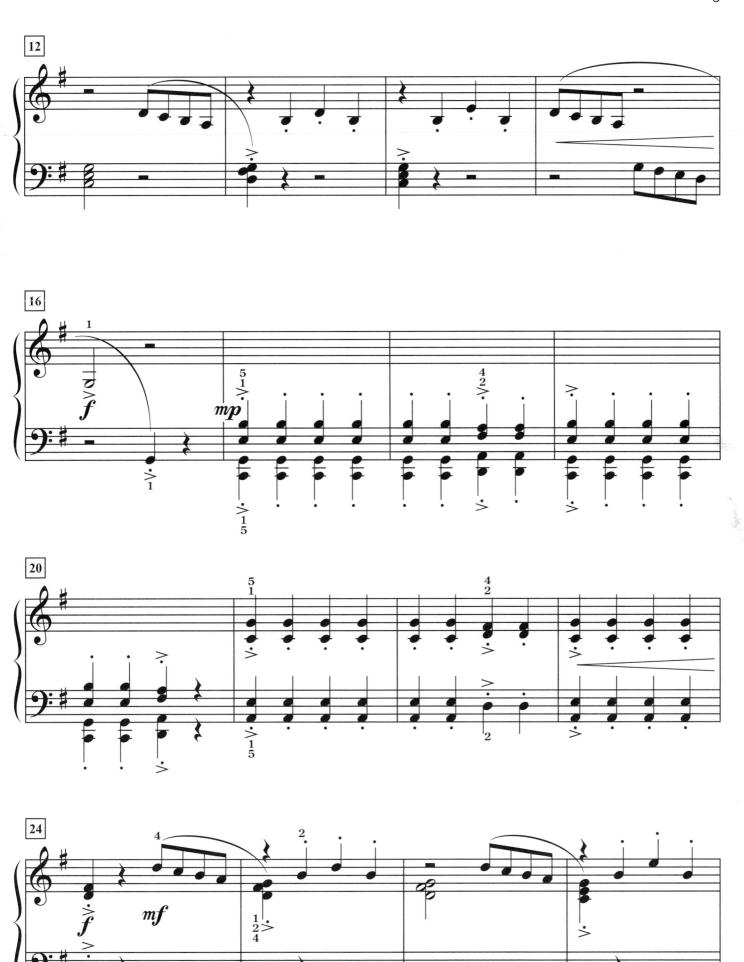

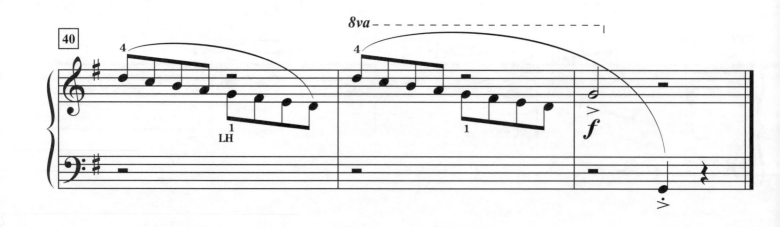

Rock Climbing

Robert D. Vandall

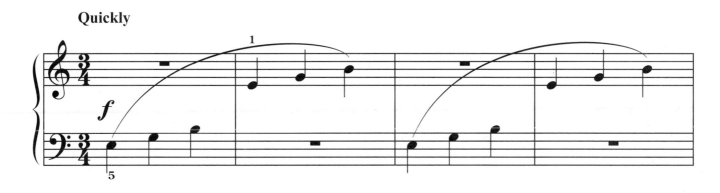

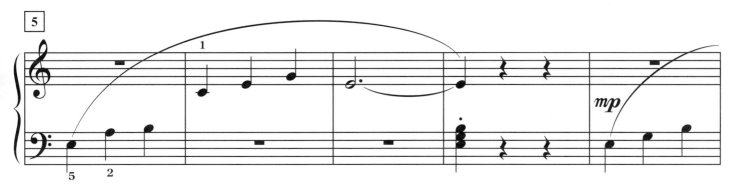

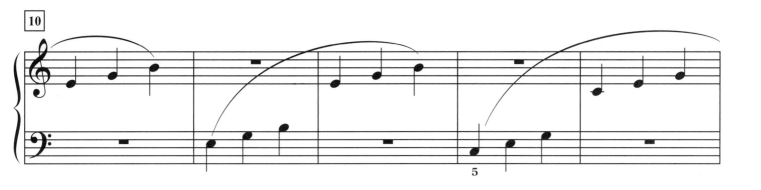

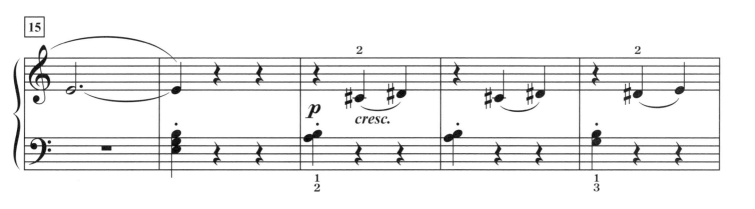

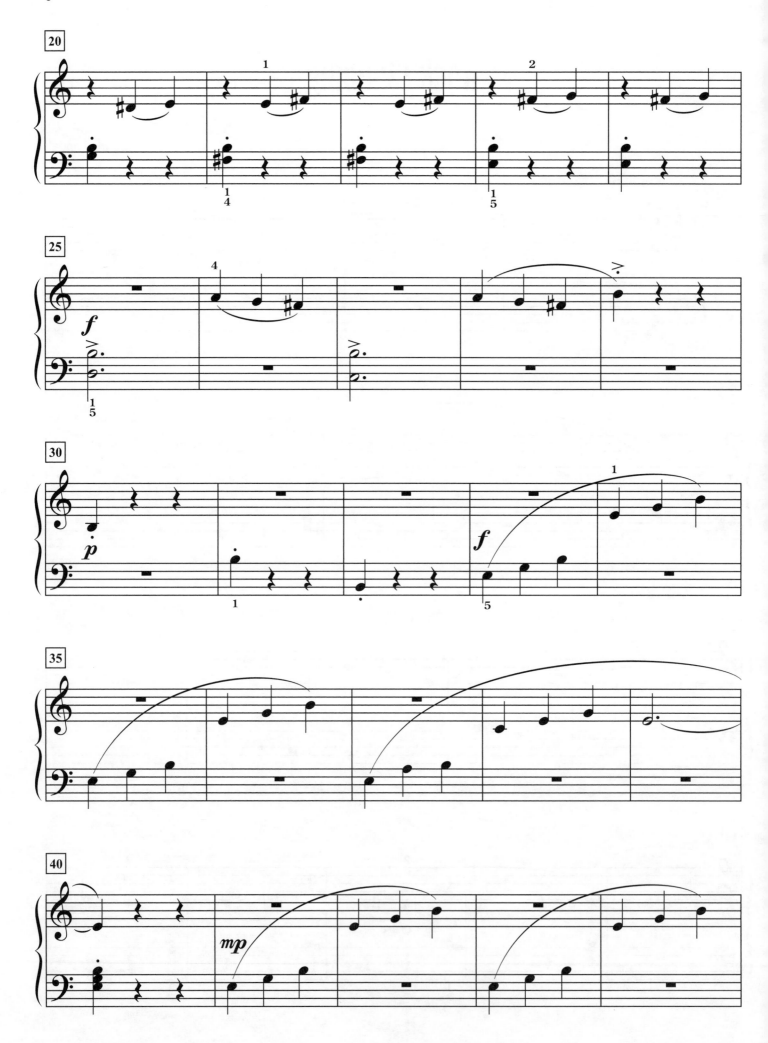

Nimble Fingers

Robert D. Vandall

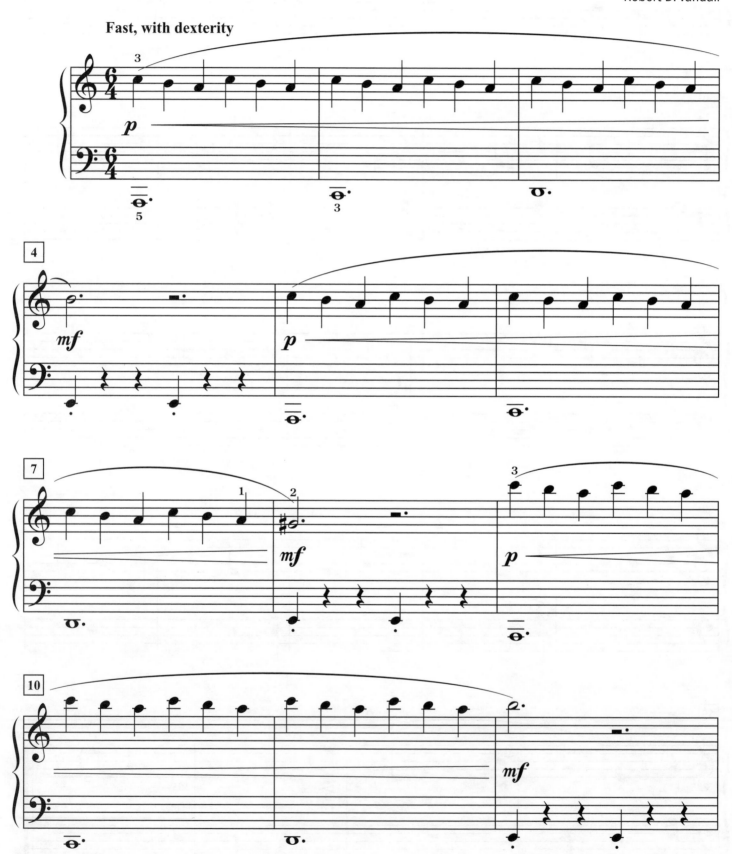

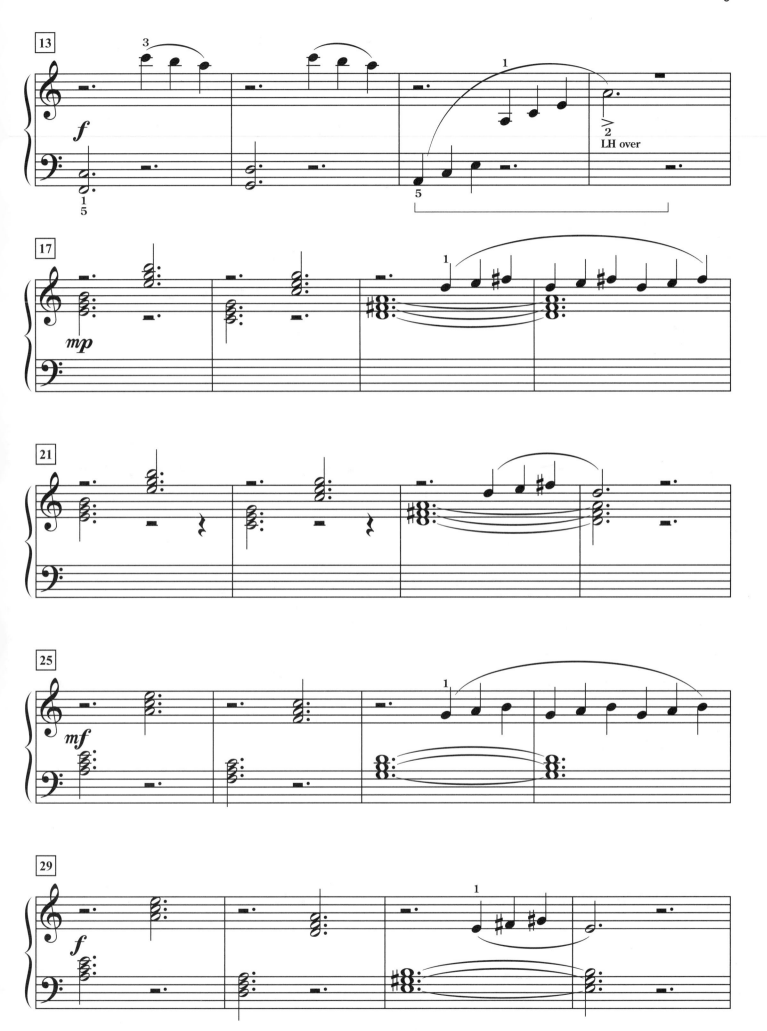

Jumping Jacks

Robert D. Vandall

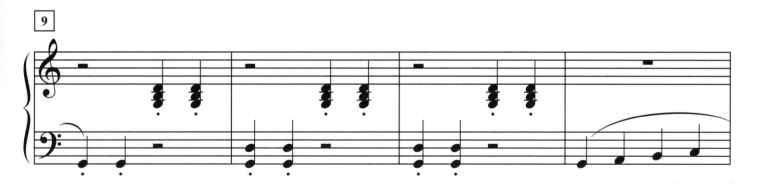

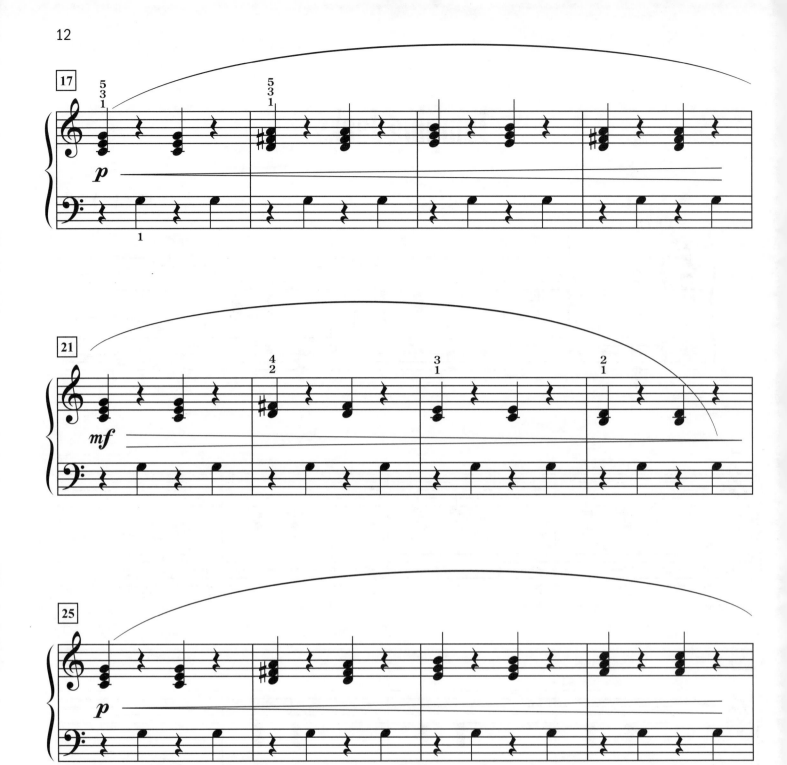

Power Walk

Robert D. Vandall

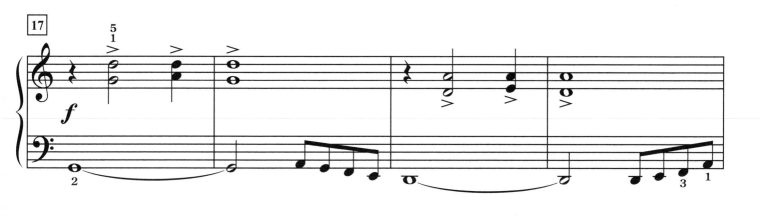

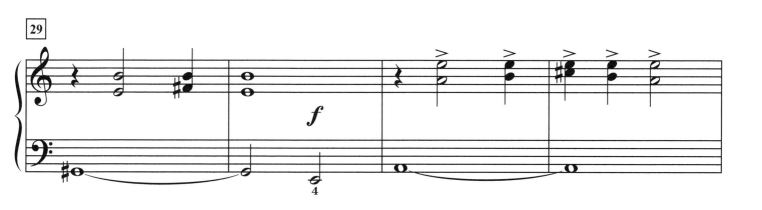

Sidewalk Games

Robert D. Vandall

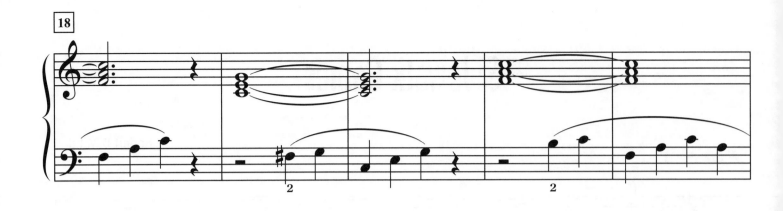

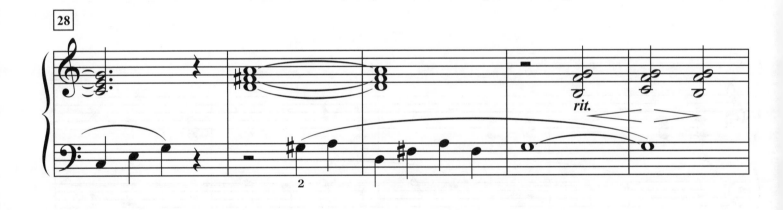

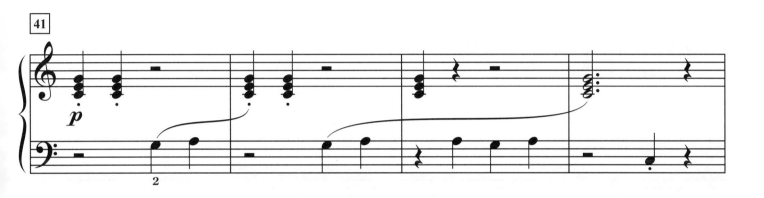

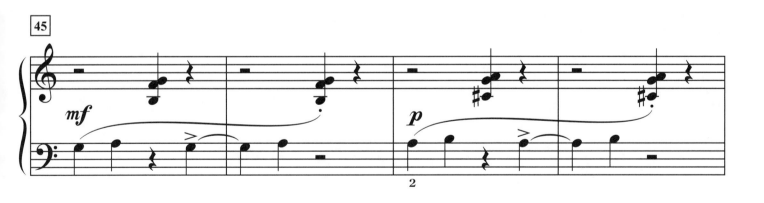

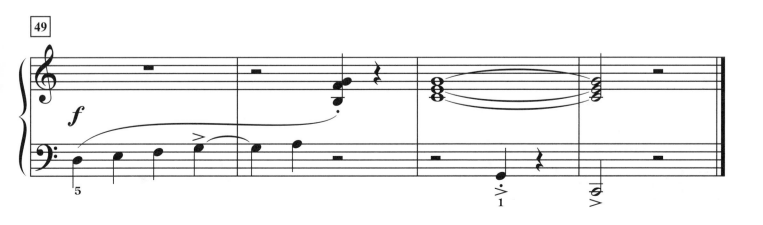

Bouncing Along

Robert D. Vandall

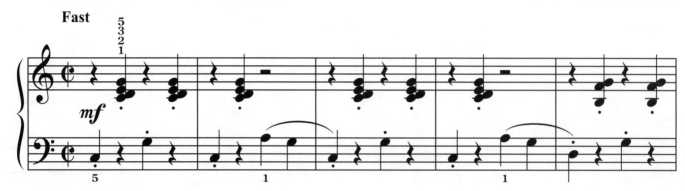

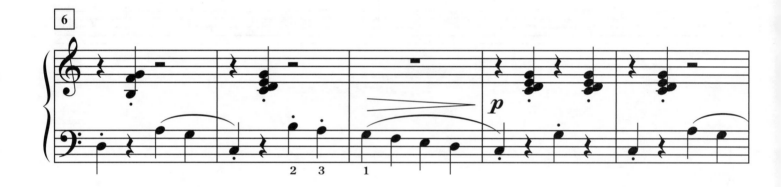

Rowdy!

Robert D. Vandall

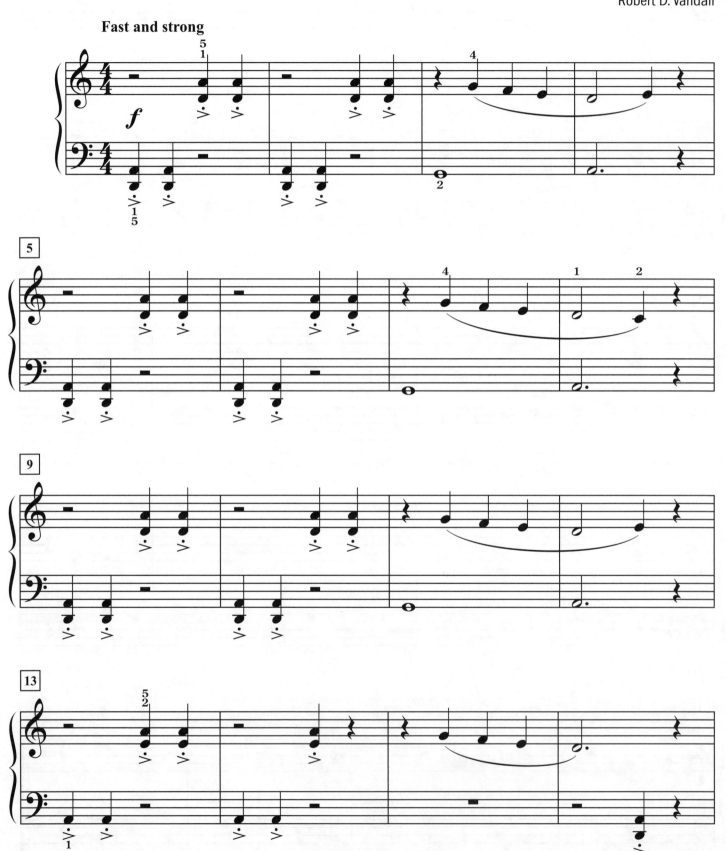

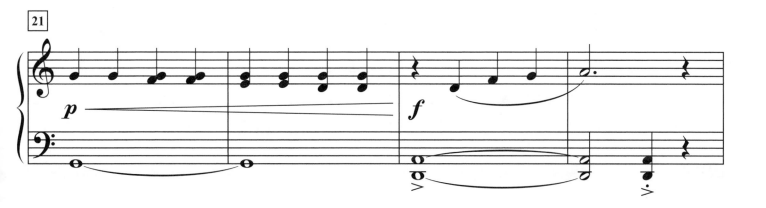

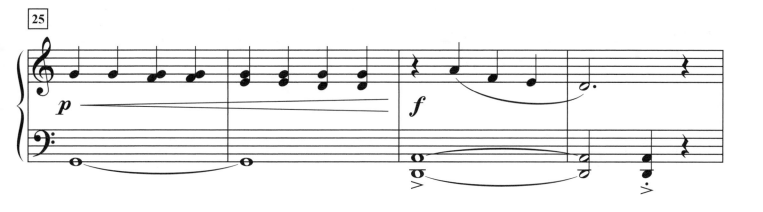

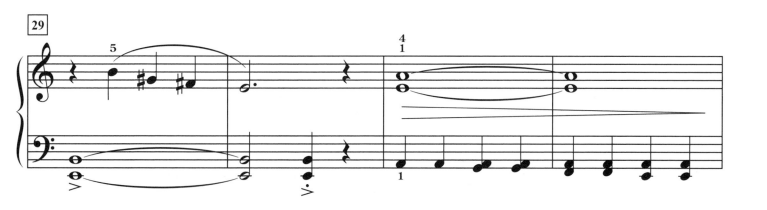